TEACHING BIBLE TRUTHS WITH A

Celebrate!

THE NAMES OF JESUS

by Dorla Schlitt

©1999 by Dorla Schlitt

All rights reserved

Published by Broadman & Holman Publishers

Nashville, Tennessee

Printed in the United States of America

0805408258

Unless otherwise stated, Scripture taken from the Holy Bible, New International Version, copyright 1973, 1978, 1984 International Bible Society. Used by permission of Zondervan Bible Publishers.

Scripture marked KJV is from the King James Version of the Bible.

Table of Contents

THEME	ACTIVITY	PAGE
JESUS	Plaster Plaque	4
THE CHRIST	Special Glasses	6
SON OF GOD	Crowns	9
SAVIOR	Geometric Design	13
LAMB OF GOD	Sparkling Globe	15
OUR PASSOVER LAMB	Communion Poster	17
LION OF JUDAH	Lion T-shirt	20
KING OF KINGS AND LORD OF LORDS	Simple Mobile	23
THE ROCK	Paperweight	26
THE GOOD SHEPHERD	Panoramic Shepherd Scene	28
THE BREAD OF LIFE	Salvation Necklace	32
THE LIGHT OF THE WORLD	Candle Bookmark	34
THE TRUE VINE	Scripture Hanging	37
THE RESURRECTION AND THE LIFE	Decorated Flower Pot	40
THE BRIGHT AND MORNING STAR	Sun Catcher	42
THE WAY, THE TRUTH, AND THE LIFE	Doily Hanging	46
OTHER RESOURCES		48

Broadman & Holman grants the buyer permission to reproduce the activity pages contained within for classroom use only. Any other use requires written permission from Broadman & Holman.

The Names of Jesus

DEAR PARENTS AND TEACHERS,

Long ago in Bible times names were very important.

Parents named their children after their family or according to the child's personality or character traits. Sometimes circumstances surrounding the child's birth determined his name. Names were important because they revealed something significant about the individual.

When you begin to study the names of Jesus with your children it is important that they know that each name, specific reference, or title given Him reveals something about His character and what He is like. It is also important for your children to know that Jesus reveals through His character what God, the Father, is like in character (John 14:9).

Although it may seem an overwhelming task to explain the character of our God to our children it is also an awesome opportunity. Begin by taking the simple truth of God's written Word and sharing it with your children. Then, pray and believe that the Holy Spirit will give each child not only insight and basic understanding of the names of Jesus but more importantly the Holy Spirit will give each child revelation of who Jesus is to them personally through His names.

My prayers are with you as you lead your children.

In His Holy Name,
Dorla Schlitt

Jesus

PLASTER PLAQUE

Appropriately, the first name you'll want to study with your children is "JESUS." Explain to your children that "Jesus" is His personal name just as each of them have a personal name.

Read Matthew 1:18-25 and Luke 1:26-38 with your children to discover how Jesus came to be named "Jesus" and what additional truth was revealed to Mary and Joseph about their son.

"Jesus" in Hebrew means "Joshua" and was a very common name in those times. It is interesting and important to consider the fact that God did not give His Son an imposing or lofty name but chose to reveal Himself (Colossians 1:15) through a human being with a name that was approachable. And, just like His name, the man, Jesus, was the kind of person that people would come to without fear of being turned away.

Take some time to talk with your children about the person, Jesus. Share with them stories from the Bible of people coming to Jesus with their needs. Assure your children that Jesus understands them and cares about them. Just as He was gentle, kind, patient, and forgiving with those who came to Him while He walked the earth so is He today.

Hebrews 13:8 tells us "Jesus Christ is the same yesterday and today and forever."

She will give birth to a son, and you are to give him the name Jesus, because he will save his people from their sins.
Matthew 1:21

Jesus went through all the towns and villages, teaching in their synagogues, preaching the good news of the kingdom and healing every disease and sickness.
Matthew 9:35

Jesus said, "Let the little children come to me, and do not hinder them, for the kingdom of heaven belongs to such as these."
Matthew 19:14

Thank You, Jesus, that You understand me and I can come to You anytime anywhere. Thank You that You are always there for me and are so willing to help me.

JESUS (CONTINUED)

materials

- gallon wax milk carton
- tempera paints
- small bag of plaster of paris
- paintbrushes
- large plastic bowl
- water
- paint stirrer
- newspaper
- clear glossy fixative spray
- 2 large paper clips
- small piece fine grain sandpaper
- ruler
- pencil
- black fine tip marker
- scissors
- felt square

preparation

1. Cover the work area with newspaper.
2. Place at the work area: water, plaster of paris, paint stirrer, large plastic bowl, and paper clips.
3. Measure, mark, and cut down the sides of the wax milk carton leaving only a 1" rim.

procedure

1. Mix according to package directions an appropriate amount of plaster of paris to fill the wax milk carton.
2. Pour the mixture into the wax carton and fill it to the rim. Smooth the surface.
3. Carefully and evenly place the 2 large paper clips into the plaster of paris with the tips only overhanging the rim for easy hanging. Let harden.
4. Carefully remove the hardened plaster of paris from the milk carton mold.
5. Use the fine grain sandpaper to smooth any rough areas.
6. Paint the back and sides of the plaster surface a solid color. Let dry. Paint the top of the plaster surface. Let dry.
7. Measure, mark, and cut felt to cover the back of the plaster plaque. Glue in place.
8. Using a pencil neatly print "Jesus" in large letters on the top surface.
9. Go over the penciled letters with a fine tip black marker.
10. Decorate the border.

The Christ

SPECIAL GLASSES

"Who do you say that I am?" Jesus asked His disciples this question long ago and still asks it today. Many responded: a teacher (John 3:2), a prophet (Matthew 21:11), a friend of sinners (Matthew 11:19), the carpenter's son (Matthew 13:55). All these responses are true. By outward appearance Jesus was all of these and more. However, Jesus was providing the opportunity for a different kind of response and Peter was the one to reply. Peter said, "Thou art the Christ, the Son of the living God."

To understand the importance of Peter's response read with your children Matthew 16:13-17. Peter's response showed that he believed Jesus to be more than just a man. Peter had received a revelation from God as to Jesus' true identity. He recognized Jesus as God in the flesh, the Son of the living God.

God wants each of us to come to know Jesus Christ for who He truly is and to believe in Him for our salvation. We cannot depend on our parent's faith, our church's teaching, or our friend's opinions to gain salvation. We must come ourselves. We must first recognize that Jesus, the Christ, was set apart and sent by God for the redemption of all mankind. Then we need to individually acknowledge our need for a savior and receive Him by faith into our heart.

Use the special glasses in this activity to do an experiment. Use them to look at the name design. As they look through the glasses they will only see the name "Jesus." This is similar to what the Holy Spirit does when we read God's word. He enables the reader to see the person of Jesus Christ, the Son of the living God!

Simon Peter answered, "You are the Christ, the Son of the living God." Matthew 16:16

Jesus, who is called Christ. Matthew 1:16

God has made this Jesus,...both Lord and Christ. Acts 2:36

Everyone who believes that Jesus is the Christ is born of God. I John 5:1

Thank You, Jesus, for sending the Holy Spirit to teach me the things of God and open my eyes to the truth of Your Word. Help me to know You and love You even more.

THE CHRIST (CONTINUED)

materials
- posterboard
- patterns
- crayons
- glue
- red cellophane
- construction paper
- scissors
- pencil
- black fine tip marker

procedure

1. Draw around the patterns on poster board and cut out.
2. Measure and cut enough red cellophane to completely cover the eye piece. Glue in place. Trim excess.
3. Place the second poster board eye piece over the first covering the rough edges of cellophane. Glue in place.
4. Use the black fine tip marker to print the name "Jesus".
5. Draw and color a bright design on the construction paper over and around the name "Jesus".
6. Wear the special glasses and notice the design.
7. What happens to the design? What do you notice about the name "Jesus"?

view with glasses

GLASSES PATTERN

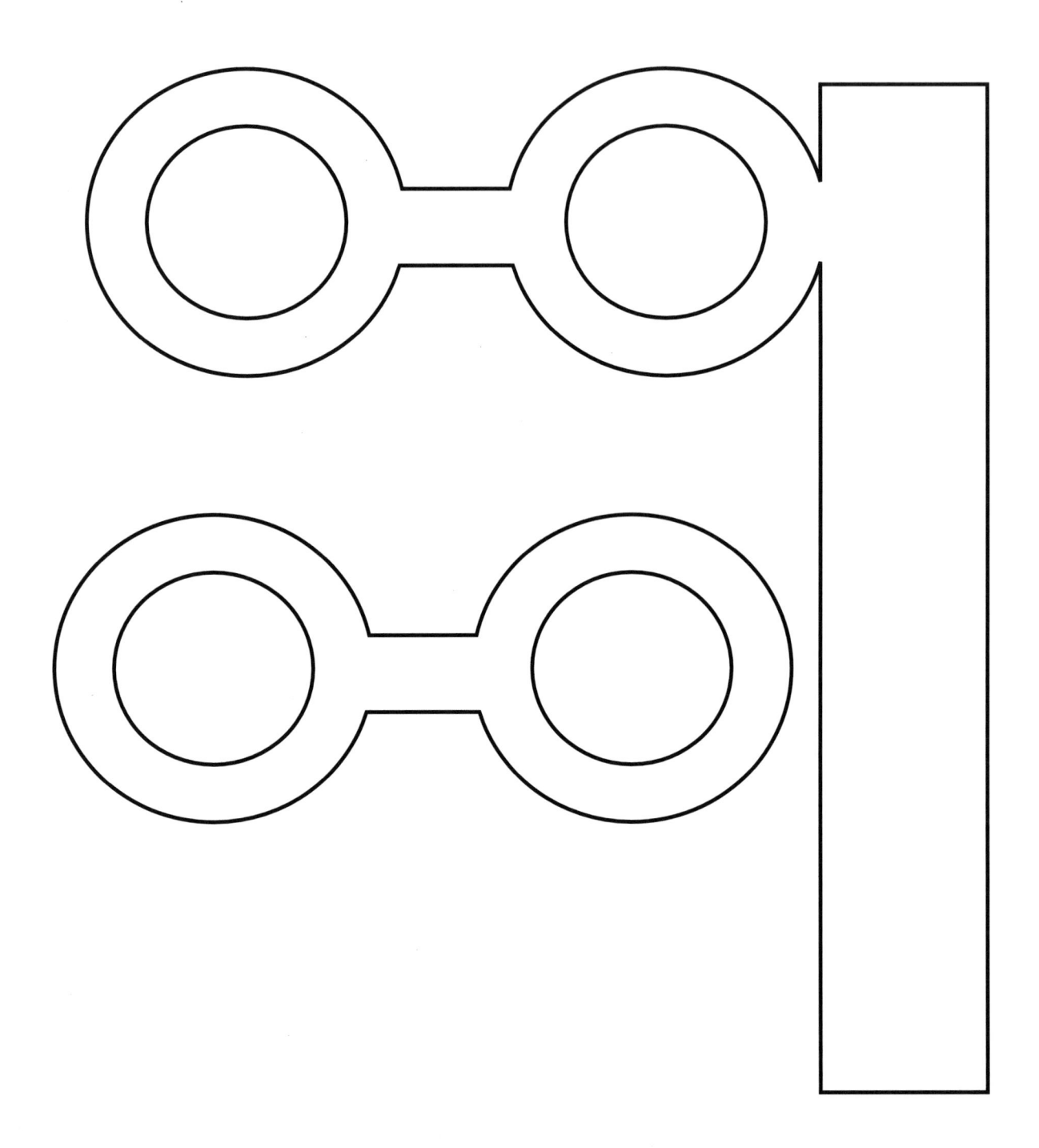

8

Son of God

CROWNS

Constructing a crown is a simple yet fun activity for all ages. It also provides an opportunity to talk with your children about the Son of God, Jesus.

Begin your discussion by explaining that a crown can be as simple as a garland or wreath worn on the head or as ornate as a heavily jeweled circlet.

Throughout history, crowns have been worn by kings and monarchs as emblems of honor and sovereignty or absolute power and authority.

Although children are usually accustomed to referring to Jesus as "Savior" it is important they also recognize His Lordship. Acts 10:36 tells us Jesus Christ is "Lord of all." "Lord" means "ruler, master". Revelation 17:14 tells us Jesus is "King of kings and Lord of lords".

When Jesus was brought before Pilate, He was asked many questions. Because He was a Jew and He spoke of a kingdom, evil men mocked Him. The soldiers even twisted a crown of thorns and put it on His head. They put a purple robe on Him and jeered, "Hail! King of the Jews!"

Little did these men realize that the man they had crowned with thorns is the same man they would someday bow their knee to and acknowledge as Lord. They will recognize, as all men will, that Jesus is Lord and He is crowned with glory and honor!

The LORD is King for ever and ever. Psalm 10:16

*Which God will bring about in his own time–
God, the blessed and only Ruler, the King of kings and Lord of lords.
1 Timothy 6:15*

Lord, You are the King of all things. We praise You for the love with which You rule the world. Thank You for a love that never ends.

CROWNS (CONTINUED)

materials

- 12" x 18" construction paper
- trims
- sequins
- buttons
- yarns
- glitter
- ribbons
- aluminum foil
- glue
- scissors
- stapler
- pencil
- 3 crown patterns
- insert pattern

procedure

1. Let each child choose which crown pattern he or she would like to use.
2. Fold the 12" x 18" construction paper sheet in half.
3. Place the crown patterns on the construction paper matching fold line to fold.
4. Draw around the crown and insert patterns. Cut them out.
5. Decorate the crown.
6. Use the insert to adjust to the head size. Staple.

12"

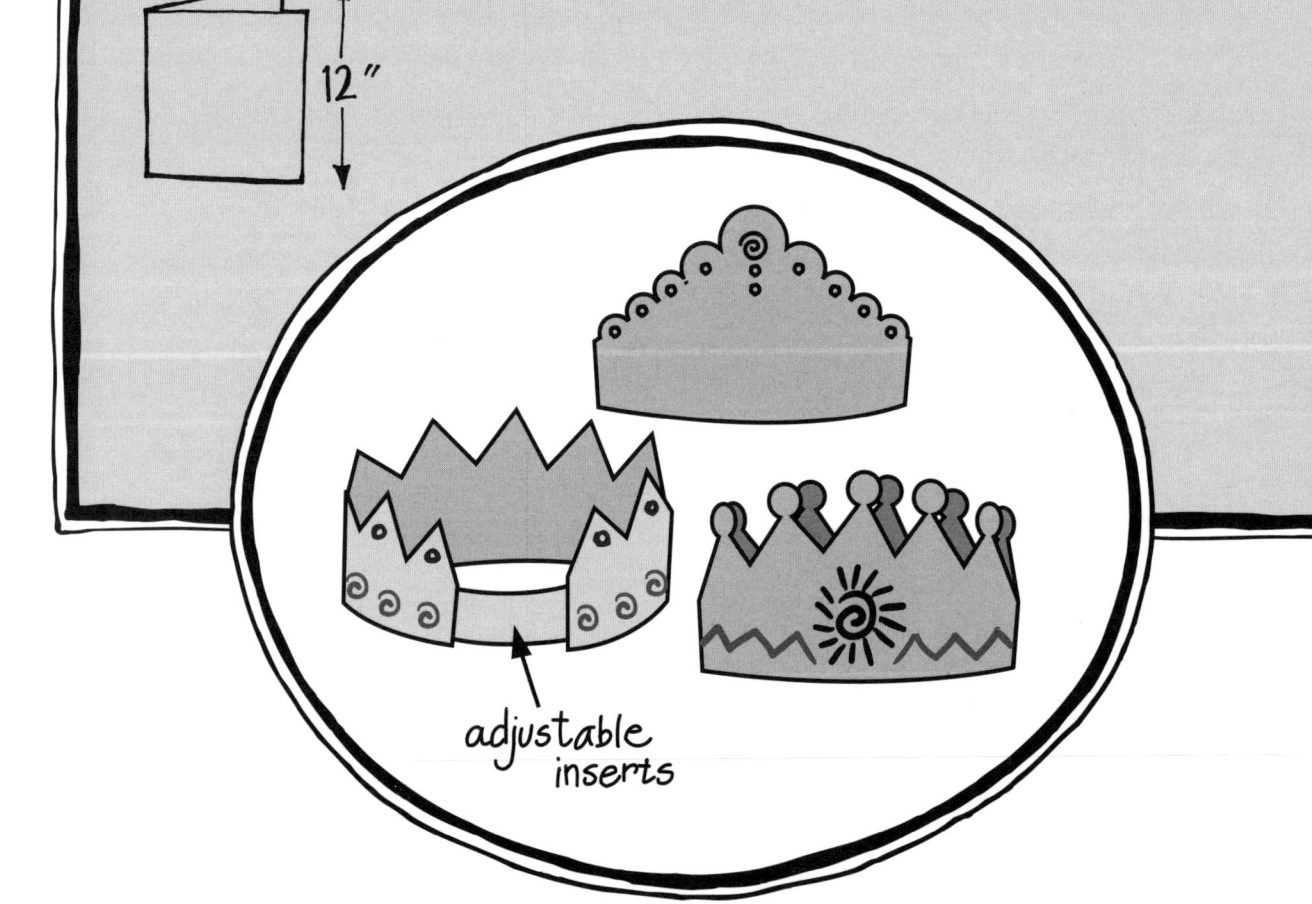

adjustable inserts

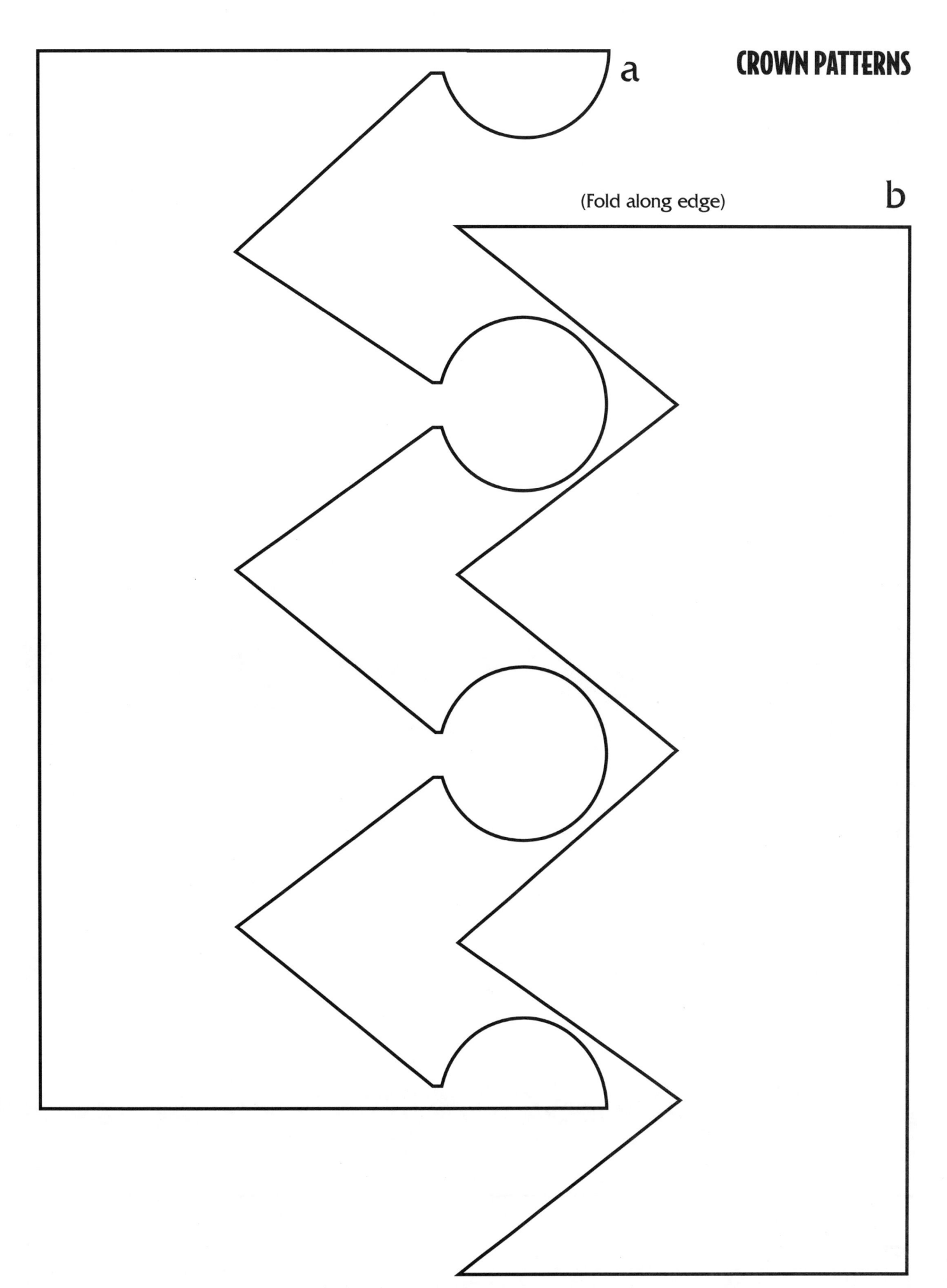

CROWN PATTERNS

a

b

(Fold along edge)

CROWN PATTERNS (CONTINUED)

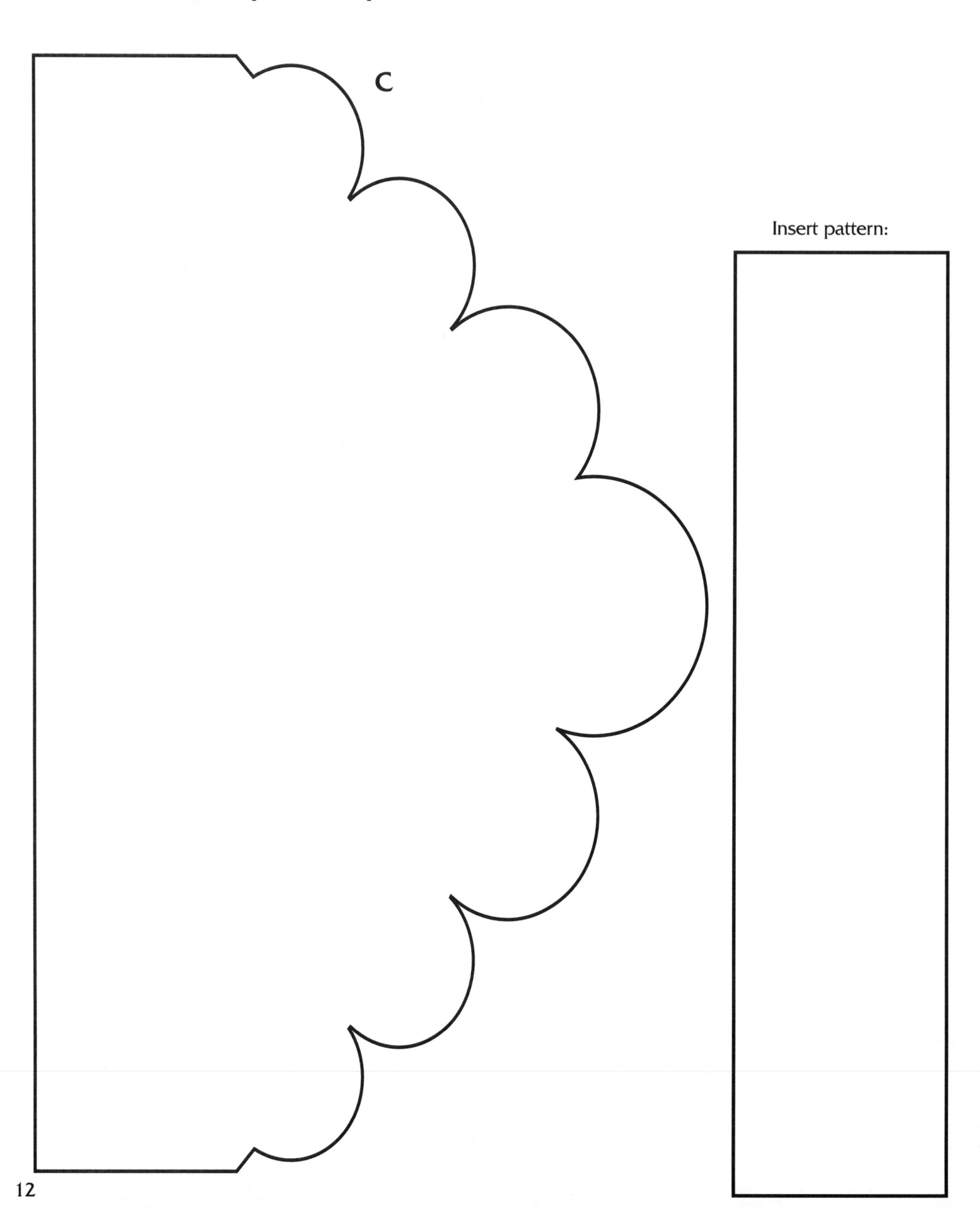

C

Insert pattern:

12

Savior

GEOMETRIC DESIGN

What a wonderful announcement the angels brought to the shepherds the night Jesus was born! The long awaited Savior had come!

From the time Adam and Eve had sinned in the garden and throughout the Old Testament, God spoke through His prophets that at some appointed, foreordained time in history He would send a Savior.

In Hebrew, the language of the Old Testament, "savior" meant one who rescues or brings salvation. In Greek, the language of the New Testament, "savior" refers to a deliverer, one who saves or delivers.

Although God's prophets foretold specific information concerning the coming Savior's birth, life, and death, the majority of people at that time failed to accept Jesus as the One God had promised.

The Jewish people were hoping for a political leader to deliver them from Roman rule and be their king (Luke 24:21). They wanted a savior who would rescue them and provide for their physical needs (John 6:14).

Although Jesus continually attended to the physical needs of people He was most concerned for their spiritual needs. After all it was for the spiritual needs of all mankind that He had come.

Tell the story of the Samaritan woman found in John 4:1-42. The Samaritan woman came to the well to gather water for her household. However, when she approached the well, she quite unexpectedly had a personal encounter with Jesus. He spoke to her of spiritual things that she did not fully understand and revealed to her His identity as Messiah, or Savior. Upon leaving His presence she quickly went about sharing with other Samaritans what she had experienced. As a result of her testimony many others came to believe in Jesus.

The Jewish people looked down on the Samaritans and found them unacceptable to God. However, this woman, a Samaritan, talked with Jesus and received a revelation of Jesus' true identity - Savior of ALL mankind!

Today in the town of David a Savior has been born to you; he is Christ the Lord. Luke 2:11

We no longer believe just because of what you said; now we have heard for ourselves, and we know that this man really is the Savior of the world. John 4:42

We wait for the blessed hope– the glorious appearing of our great God and Savior, Jesus Christ, who gave himself for us to redeem us from all wickedness and to purify for himself a people that are his very own. Titus 2:13-14

Thank You, Jesus, that just as You spoke to the Samaritan woman who was thought to be unacceptable to God, You speak to each of us and reveal Yourself as Savior so that we might receive You and become acceptable to God. Thank You for Your love and mercy towards us.

GEOMETRIC DESIGN (CONTINUED)

materials

- construction paper: red, black, white
- glue
- pencil
- scissors
- fine tip black marker
- ruler
- compass

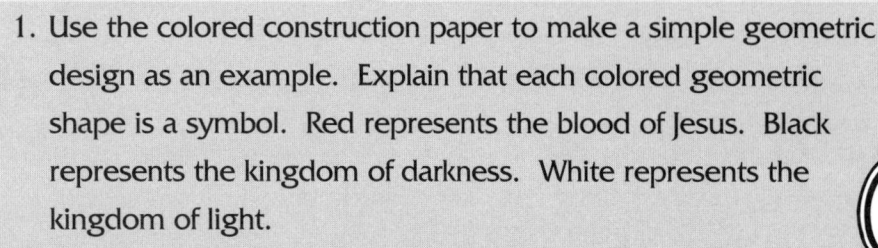

procedure

1. Use the colored construction paper to make a simple geometric design as an example. Explain that each colored geometric shape is a symbol. Red represents the blood of Jesus. Black represents the kingdom of darkness. White represents the kingdom of light.
2. Choose a color to use as the background sheet for your design.
3. Using a ruler and compass draw and cut out large geometric shapes from the other two colors of construction paper.
4. Overlap and overlay the geometric shapes on the background color making a geometric design. Keep it simple.
5. Somewhere on the design neatly print in pencil Colossians 1:13-14. Trace over the pencil with the black marker.
6. Display the designs side-by-side.

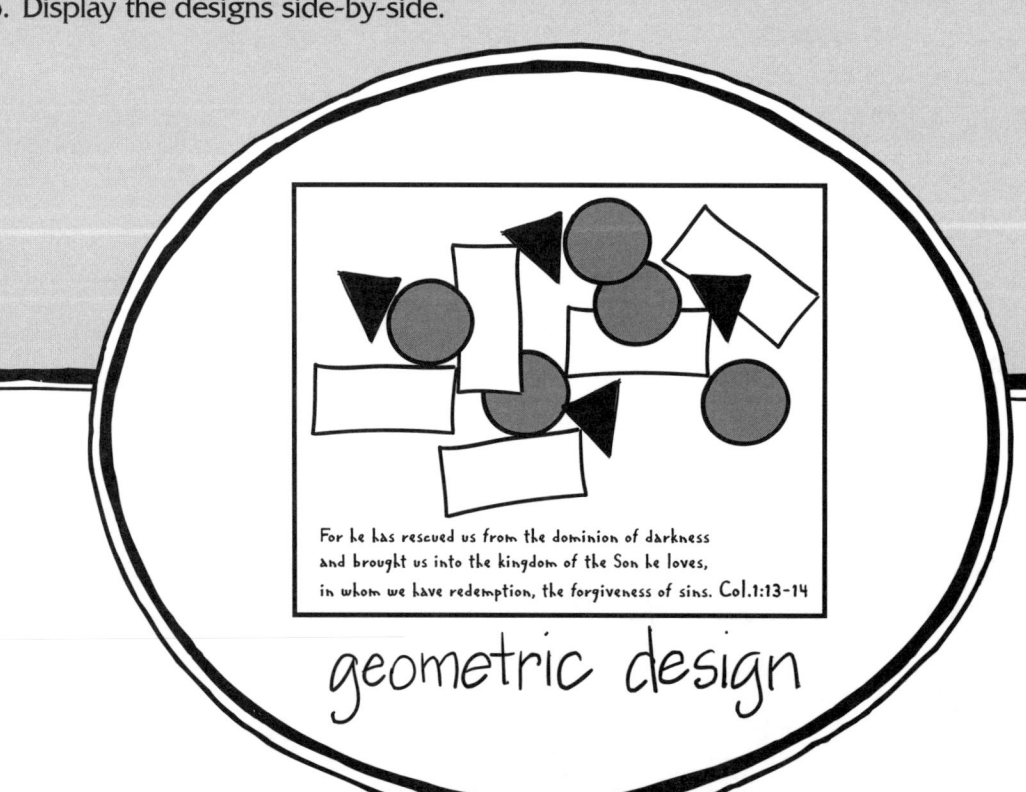

For he has rescued us from the dominion of darkness and brought us into the kingdom of the Son he loves, in whom we have redemption, the forgiveness of sins. Col.1:13-14

geometric design

Lamb of God

A SPARKLING GLOBE

purpose

The word Lamb, referring to Jesus, is very significant. Not only is Jesus gentle and meek in spirit like a lamb, but He was also innocent of any wrongdoing. Jesus was without sin yet He gave His life and shed His blood for the redemption of all mankind. His blood completely paid the price for the penalty of sin.

In the Old Testament, the Jewish people sacrificed a lamb to pay for their sins that stood between them and a relationship with God. Jesus willingly became the sacrifice for our sins so we could come to a new relationship with God. As a result of Jesus' sacrifice the old covenant was replaced with a new and better covenant between God and man. This new covenant is entered into by faith in believing and accepting Jesus Christ as your Savior.

Jesus, the Lamb of God, is worthy of our thankfulness, our praise, and our worship!

scripture

*John saw Jesus coming toward him and said,
"Look, the Lamb of God, who takes away the sin of the world!"
John 1:29*

*Worthy is the Lamb, who was slain, to receive power and wealth
and wisdom and strength and honor and glory and praise!
Revelation 5:12*

prayer

Thank You, Jesus that You are the Lamb of God. Thank You for being so kind and gentle. Thank You for being willing to give Your life and shed Your blood for me and the forgiveness of my sin.

LAMB OF GOD (CONTINUED)

materials

- small plastic lamb
- small silk flowers
- blossoms/leaves
- red glitter
- red satin ribbon
- craft sticks
- baby oil
- wide mouth clear glass olive jar & lid
- low heat glue gun & glue sticks
- black fine tip marker
- kitchen cutting board
- scissors

procedure

1. Place the kitchen cutting board in a safe work space near an electrical outlet.
2. Plug in the glue gun and load with a glue stick. Lay it on the cutting board.

1. Use the glue gun to securely anchor the small plastic lamb to the inside of the jar lid. Let dry.
2. Using the scissors and the craft sticks measure, cut, and glue two appropriately sized pieces together to form a cross. It must fit inside the jar beside the lamb.
3. Print ìJesusî on the horizontal piece of the cross. Glue the cross in place.
4. Arrange and glue in place the small silk flower blossoms/leaves around the base of the cross and lamb. Be sure they are within the boundary of the lid rim.
5. Pour some red glitter into the empty clear glass jar.
6. Fill the jar to the rim with baby oil. Secure the lid.
7. Carefully apply a line of warm glue around the rim of the jar.
8. Cut a length of satin ribbon long enough to wrap around the outside rim of the lid and make a small bow.
9. Invert the jar and watch the glitter fall through the oil to the base of the jar.

finished globe

Our Passover Lamb

COMMUNION POSTER

purpose

This simple craft provides an opportunity for you to teach your children about an important festival or celebration the Israelites in the Old Testament observed and how it has significance for us today in our understanding of Jesus as our Passover Lamb and the Lord's Supper, commonly called "communion." The observance of Passover in the Old Testament and the Lord's Supper in the New Testament are times of remembrance, thankfulness, and joy. In observing the yearly Passover celebration the Hebrew people of the Old Testament were thankful and joyful. They remembered God's deliverance of the Israelite people in Egypt from death as the death angel saw the blood of the lamb on their doorposts and "passed over" them. The Passover celebration was also a joyful time for the Hebrew people as they looked forward to their future as God's children and the blessings of being in convenant with Him.

In partaking of the Lord's Supper we, too, are to be thankful and joyful. We should be thankful for what Jesus did for us in delivering us from sin and death. It is also a joyful celebration of looking forward to continued fellowship and communion with God through Jesus Christ, of learning more about Him and who we are as His children, and of looking forward to His return. Celebrate Jesus, our Passover Lamb!

scripture

For Christ, our Passover lamb, has been sacrificed.
I Corinthians 5:7

Do this in remembrance of me.
Luke 22:19

prayer

Thank You, Jesus, for being our Passover Lamb. Help me as I take communion to remember and be thankful that You paid the complete and final price for sin—my sin. You died in my place so that I wouldn't have to die. I look forward to knowing You more and being Your child. I look forward to Your return!

OUR PASSOVER LAMB (CONTINUED)

materials

- large poster board
- patterns
- pencil
- scissors
- glue
- small brown paper bag
- foil
- ruler
- construction paper: green, yellow, blue or purple
- black fine tip marker

procedure

1. Cut the poster board into 4 equal sections. Use one for this project.
2. Crumple a small brown bag. Smooth it out. Draw around the bread pattern and cut it out.
3. Draw around the goblet pattern on the foil. Cut it out.
4. Draw around the grape pattern on the blue or purple paper. Cut them out.
5. Draw around the leaf patterns on the green paper. Cut them out.
6. Fold the yellow paper several times. Draw around the oval pattern on the yellow paper. Cut out the oval shape making several at a time. Make enough to form an overlapping border around the poster board edge making a frame.
7. Arrange the goblet, bread, grapes, and leaves on the posterboard. Glue in place.
8. Using the ruler draw two light pencil lines at the top of the poster. Neatly print in pencil Luke 22:19. Trace over the pencil in black fine tip marker.

communion poster

COMMUNION PATTERNS

19

Lion of Judah

LION T-SHIRT

Read Revelation 5:5. Jesus as the Lion of Judah reveals more of Jesus' character. What are the characteristics of a lion's nature? Strength, boldness, and courage are three important qualities of a lion's nature. The lion is often thought of as the king of the jungle for he is very majestic in his manner.

As the lion of Judah, Jesus represents superior courage, strength, and power. He defeated Satan (Colossians 2:15) and brings people of every tribe, nation, and language into His kingdom, the kingdom of God (Revelation 5:9).

As the Lion of Judah, Jesus also represents absolute justice and authority. He is the King of kings and Lord of lords (I Timothy 6:15). Jesus, the Lion of Judah, will reign forever!

purpose

The Lion of the tribe of Judah,...has triumphed.
Revelation 5:5

With justice he (Jesus) judges.
Revelation 19:11

Behold, I am coming soon!
Revelation 22:7

scripture

Thank You, Jesus, that because I know You as my Savior, the Lamb of God, I will never fear You as my judge. I thank You that I can look forward to Your return as the Lion of Judah and to being with You forever.

prayer

LION OF JUDAH (CONTINUED)

materials

- acrylic paint: brown, light brown
- bottle textile medium
- prewashed white T-shirt
- sponges
- margarine container and lid
- 10"x18" posterboard
- newspaper
- paper towels
- 20mm movable eyes
- fabric glue
- pencil
- black fine tip paint marker or permanent marker
- red paint marker or permanent marker
- 1/2" - 3/4" paintbrush
- lion face pattern

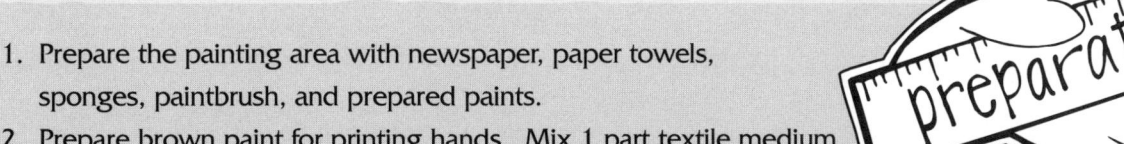

preparation

1. Prepare the painting area with newspaper, paper towels, sponges, paintbrush, and prepared paints.
2. Prepare brown paint for printing hands. Mix 1 part textile medium to 2 parts acrylic paint on one margarine lid. Prepare the light brown paint following the same directions. Use the margarine container as the child will need a lot of paint to cover the T-shirt surface. The shirt will absorb the paint quickly.
3. Prepare the clean up area if you do not have a sink.
4. Prepare an area to hang or lay the finished T-shirt
5. Cut sponge squares to spread paint.
6. Insert the poster board into the T-shirt to prevent the paint from bleeding through.
7. Prepare the lion face pattern.
   If you are working with a group of children have them gather around you to watch as you demonstrate the activity before they begin.

procedure

1. Using a pencil to draw around the lion face pattern on the T-shirt front. Be sure to center the face.
2. At the paint table the child will use the paintbrush and light brown paint to paint the face of the lion. The paint is absorbed quickly into the fabric. Be sure the paint completely fills the space. Dry several hours.
3. To make the lion's mane the child will paint one hand brown using the sponge dipped in brown paint. Do not paint too thickly.
4. Begin at the top of the lion's face on the T-shirt front.
5. Direct their hand and lay it flat on the T-shirt and press.
6. Repeat the procedure moving around the outside of the face and overlapping the hand prints to make a full lioní's mane. Let dry thoroughly for several hours.
7. When dry, glue the movable eyes in place.
8. Use the pencil to lightly draw the lion's nose, ears, jowls, and eyebrows.
9. Trace over the pencil drawing of each with a fine tip black paint marker or permanent marker. Fill in the nose with black paint and draw whiskers.
10. Trace over the mouth of the lion with the red paint marker or permanent marker and fill in the space.
11. Neatly print in pencil over the top and underneath the lion face: Jesus, the Lion of Judah will reign forever! Trace over the pencil with the black fine tip paint marker or permanent marker.
12. Remove the cardboard.

PATTERN FOR LION OF JUDAH

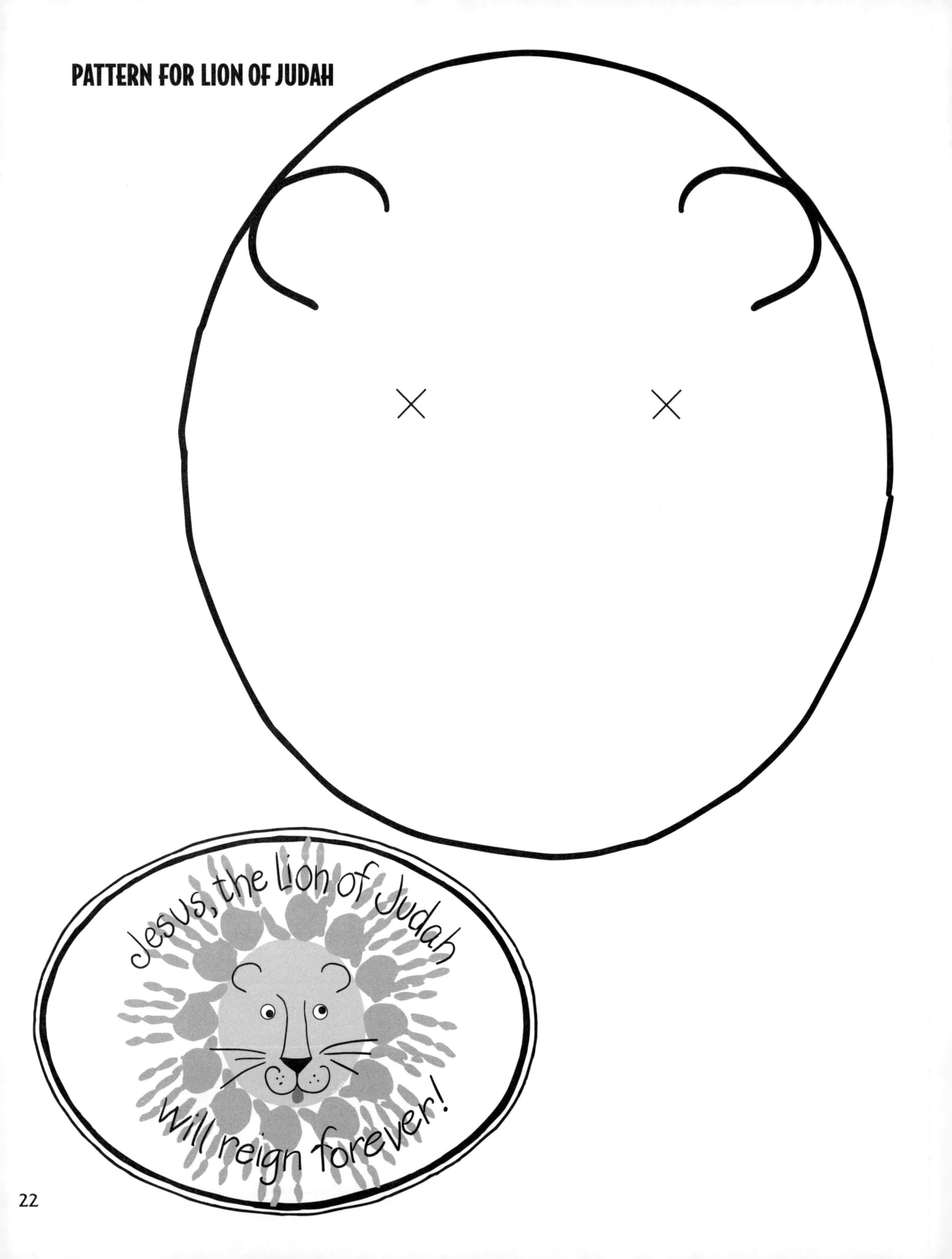

22

King of Kings and Lord of Lords

SIMPLE MOBILE

"Today in the town of David a Savior has been born to you; he is Christ the Lord." Luke 2:11 tells us that the title "Lord" was first given Jesus Christ at the time of His birth by the angels who were delivering the news to the shepherds in their fields.

What does the word "Lord" mean? The dictionary defines "Lord" as someone having a leadership relationship with others. It could be a ruler, a commander, or someone who has authority or power over another person. It also could be one who is a master over another or owner.

purpose

God wants each of us to not only accept Jesus as our personal Savior but He also wants us to acknowledge Jesus as the Lord of our lives.

As our Savior we believe and accept that Jesus died for our sins and saved us from having to pay the penalty ourselves. As Lord we recognize and accept His ownership and authority over us.

Construct this simple mobile as a reminder of Jesus' lordship over all created things.

scripture

On his robe and on his thigh he has this name written:
KING OF KINGS AND LORD OF LORDS.
Revelation 19:16

Jesus Christ, ..the blessed and only Ruler, the King of kings and Lord of lords, who alone is immortal and who lives in unapproachable light.
I Timothy 6:15

That at the name of Jesus every knee should bow in heaven and on earth and under the earth and every tongue confess that Jesus Christ is Lord, to the glory of God the Father.
Philippians 2:10-11

Thank you, Jesus, that Your Word tells me that You are Lord of all! I can rest in knowing that You are in control and that nothing can separate Your love from me.

prayer

KING OF KING AND LORD OF LORDS (CONTINUED)

materials

- 11" x 14" section of poster board
- 3 sheets of 8" x 11" construction paper
- paper punch
- large needle and sturdy thread
- pattern
- colored markers
- scissors
- glue
- crayons
- ruler
- pencil

procedure

1. Measure, mark, and punch 3 equally spaced holes approximately 1" from the bottom edge of the poster board section.
2. Measure and lightly draw 3 straight equally spaced lines on both sides of the poster board section. Neatly print in large letters: Jesus, King of kings, and Lord of lords. Go over the pencil with colored marker.
3. Punch a hole at the top center of the poster board. Cut a length of thread to hang the mobile when finished.
4. Using the pattern draw around it on the three sheets of construction paper. Cut out each one.
5. Referring to the pattern mark the dotted fold lines on the construction paper shapes.
6. On sides 1-4 of each shape draw and color illustrations depicting the theme– one shape for each: earth, sea, sky.
7. Fold along the 4 inner dotted lines forming the shape. Overlap the flap as illustrated and glue in place.
8. Fold the bottom flaps and tuck them into place.
9. Using the needle and long sturdy thread poke a hole through two top sides of the shape near the point. Draw the thread through and tie it through one of the holes at the bottom of the poster board. Repeat the procedure for the remaining two shapes. Adjust the lengths of thread to give the mobile interest.

PATTERN FOR MOBILE

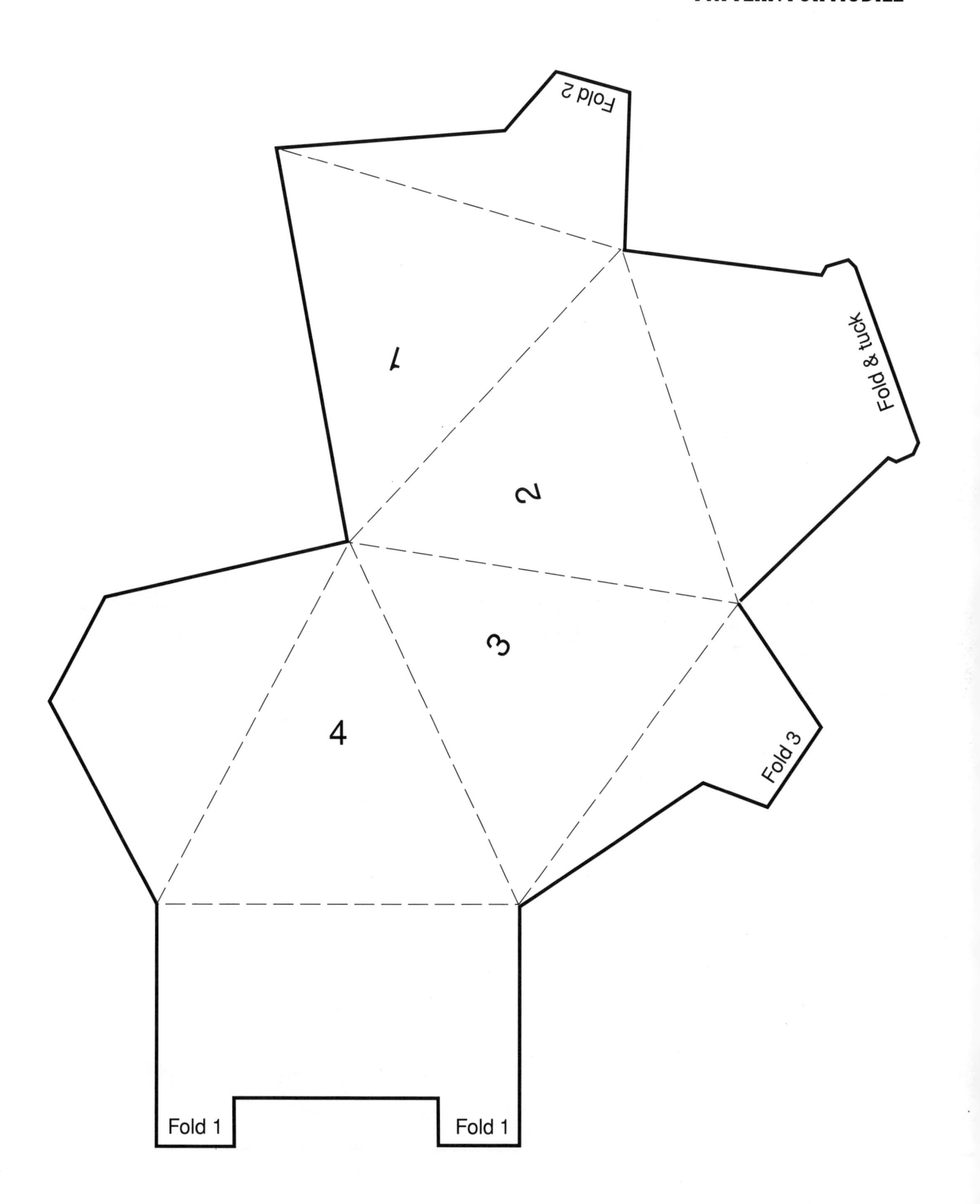

Fold 2

Fold & tuck

1

2

3

4

Fold 3

Fold 1   Fold 1

25

The ROCK

PAPERWEIGHT

Introduce this craft activity by taking a walk with your children in an area that you know has rocks of different sizes easily accessible. Everyone should look for a good paperweight-size rock that has a flat surface to rest upright. Also look for several much smaller rocks for the activity.

As you walk and search the ground share with your children the reason why you each need to find a rock of good size. Explain that they will be making a paperweight to hold their papers on their desk or dresser and also serve as a reminder to them of one of the names of Jesus—Jesus, the Rock.

There are a number of Scriptures in the Bible that refer to Jesus as "the Rock." One important reference is found in the parable of the wise and foolish builder in Matthew 7:24-27. Read this parable to your children and explain to them that Jesus is sharing an important truth about Himself and His relationship with the believer through this simple illustration.

In this parable the house represents a person's life. If a person builds their life based on a trust relationship with Jesus Christ, they have a strong foundation and strength to draw upon when they experience the tough times in life. However, if a person's faith in God is only empty words there is no true source of strength, no firm foundation to lean upon. When life seems to fall apart around them they are devastated.

Jesus wants us to know that He is the rock that we can build our lives on and cling to when everything around us is shaking. There is peace in knowing the undergirding presence of Jesus Christ in your life. Jesus is the Rock!

Upon this rock I will build my church. Matthew 16:18, KJV

That Rock was Christ. I Corinthians 10:4, KJV

But the LORD has become my fortress, and my God the rock in whom I take refuge. Psalm 94:22

Thank You, Jesus, that You are the Rock. Knowing and trusting You gives me the strength and the ability to endure the problems I have. I am encouraged when I remind myself my life and my salvation rests in You!

THE ROCK (CONTINUED)

materials

- large rock
- several smaller rocks
- felt square: green or brown
- hot glue gun & glue sticks
- tempera paints or acrylics
- thin paint brushes & water container
- newspapers, paper towels, pencil
- fine tip black marker
- clear glossy spray fixative

preparation

1. Wash the large rock and several smaller rocks to remove dirt. Dry.
2. Cover the painting area with newspapers.
3. Place painting supplies at the painting area.

procedure

1. Place the large rock upright on the felt square with the flat side down.
2. Draw around the area that rests on the felt square. Cut it out and glue it to the base of the large rock. Let dry.
3. Plug in the glue gun and load it with a glue stick. When it is warm glue two or three smaller rocks to the front, side, or back of the large rock to stabilize it and provide a comparison of size.
4. Using a pencil print on the large rock "Jesus is the Rock" or "Jesus is my Rock." Using the fine tip marker trace over the pencil.
5. Using the paint and brushes decorate the large rock.
6. Spray with fixative.

The Good Shepherd

PANORAMIC SHEPHERD SCENE

purpose

Ask most children what a shepherd does and their first and only response is: They watch sheep.

Although that is an accurate answer it is an incomplete one. There is much more to a shepherd's life than just "watching" sheep. Read Psalm 23. The Scriptures tell us that a good shepherd cares for the needs of his sheep. They must be fed daily with good food and receive fresh clean water. They require shade from the heat and shelter from storms. If they are hurt or bothered by insects they need careful attention so that they will recover. If they fall behind or wander away the shepherd will search them out for each one is special to him.

When a shepherd takes his flock out of the sheep gate each morning he leads them because he knows the way in which he wants them to go. He carries a rod and staff with him to guide the sheep and to pull them close if they begin to wander. He may also use his rod and staff to protect them from dangerous animals and plants.

The shepherd knows all about his sheep and he speaks to each one calling them by name. Each sheep knows the shepherd's voice and responds to it when called.

At night the shepherd brings his flock to the sheep gate. He counts them as they pass in to make sure each one is accounted for and then lays down in front of the gate to protect them. His constant presence is great comfort to the sheep and gives them peace so they can sleep. If necessary the shepherd will voluntarily give his life for his flock. His commitment to them is constant and total.

As our Shepherd, Jesus cares for our every need. Surely, Jesus is our Good Shepherd!

scripture

I am the good shepherd. John 10:14

The Lord is my shepherd; I shall not want. Psalm 23:1, KJV

Our Lord Jesus, that great Shepherd of the sheep.
Hebrews 13:20

prayer

Thank You, Jesus, for being my Good Shepherd. You know all about me and care for all my needs. You protectively lead me by Your Word and speak softly to my heart of Your love. I love You, Jesus!

THE GOOD SHEPHERD (CONTINUED)

materials

- 1/2 sheet blue poster board (28" x 11")
- shepherd and sheep forms
- construction paper: green, brown, white, light blue, yellow
- scissors, glue, ruler
- cotton balls, pencil, fine tip black marker

procedure

1. To make the panoramic background measure 8" from each end of the 28" poster board and fold each section to brace it in a standing position.
2. At the top use a ruler to draw a light line. Print neatly John 10:14 in pencil. Trace over the pencil in marker.
3. Glue pieces of green construction paper to form a landscape of green grass against the blue sky background.
4. Use brown and shades of green and yellow construction paper to make trees. Glue in place.
5. Use the light blue construction paper to make a stream.
6. Glue in place.
7. Cut out clouds from white construction paper. Lightly cover each with a cotton ball spread very thin. Glue in place.
8. With various scraps make flowers, butterflies, and birds.
9. Cut out and color the shepherd form. Fold along the dotted line and place in front of the landscape.
10. Cut out the sheep forms. Do not cut on the dotted lines. Use the black marker to color the eyes, nose, and hooves.
11. Lay the sheep form flat on the table and apply glue thinly to the form. Spread cotton over the form and glue in place.
12. Fold along the dotted lines so the sheep will stand up. Stand the sheep next to the shepherd.

PATTERNS FOR SHEEP

PATTERN FOR SHEPHERD

31

The Bread of Life

SALVATION NECKLACE

Mmmm! Smell the aroma of fresh baked bread! Doesn't it draw you into the kitchen and cause you to want to taste it?

This simple craft activity can provide an opportunity to talk with your children about Jesus, the Bread of Life.

When Moses led the Israelites out of Egypt into the desert the people began to grumble because they were hungry. Knowing their physical needs God provided abundantly for them. Read Exodus 16:1-35 and learn about a special bread called "manna." Manna was special because it came down from heaven fresh every morning. For forty years the Israelites gathered it daily. Now read John 6:25-59. Once again God is faithful and provides abundantly. This time, however, God provides not just for physical needs but for spiritual needs, as well. Like the manna God sent down from heaven in the Old Testament to feed His people, God sent Jesus down from heaven to give His life to the world. The physical bread of manna could only keep God's people alive for a time while Jesus offers eternal life to anyone who believes in Him. Jesus gave His life and shed His blood so that we might have life. He is the source of all life.

Though the physical bread satisfies the body's hunger and need to be nourished, Jesus satisfies our deepest hunger and meets our deepest need of knowing God's love and being right with Him. Jesus is the Bread of life!

I am the bread of life.
John 6:35

I am the living bread that came down from heaven.
John 6:51

Thank You, Jesus, that You are the Bread of life.
I believe You are God's Son sent from heaven to give Your life
and shed Your blood for me that I might receive life. I thank You
with all my heart for loving me so much!

SALVATION NECKLACE (CONTINUED)

materials

- bowl
- fork
- measuring cup
- 1 cup flour
- 1 cup salt
- water
- hemp cording
- tempera paints: red, white, yellow or brown
- toothpicks
- clear glossy spray fixative
- newspapers
- paintbrush

procedure

1. Preheat oven: 200 degrees
2. Measure the appropriate amounts of salt and flour for the amount of clay desired.
3. Carefully add a small amount of water and stir until the dough is like modeling clay.
4. Shape the dough into 8 1"balls and one thick 2" long cross.
5. Use a toothpick to make holes in the 8 balls to make beads. Use the same procedure for the cross.
6. Bake at 200 degrees. Check every 5 minutes until hard. Cool.
7. Paint 4 beads white. Paint 4 beads red. Dry.
8. Paint the cross yellow or brown. Dry.
9. Spray the beads and cross with the glossy clear fixative.
10. Measure an appropriate length of hemp cording and string the beads and cross. Tie at the neck.
11. Learn Isaiah 1:18 by heart and be ready to share it with someone who might ask about your necklace.

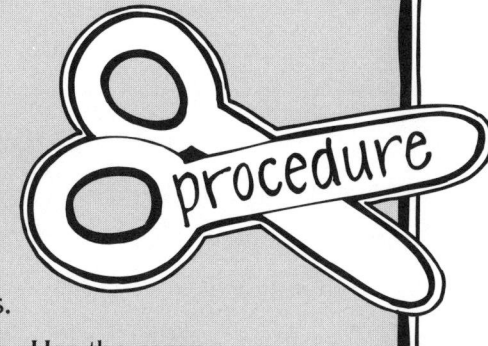

> Though your sins are like scarlet, they shall be as white as snow; though they are red as crimson, they shall be like wool.
> Isaiah 1:18

33

The Light of the World

CANDLE BOOKMARK

Use this simple craft in helping your children understand why Jesus referred to Himself as "the Light of the world."

In the very beginning, before the earth was formed, there was total darkness. Without the presence of light there is absolute darkness. Read Genesis 1:1-2,14-19, emphasizing that God provided light for the physical world. He created the sun and moon to give light on the earth. Light enables man to see all that God had for him to know and enjoy. All of God's creation is a witness of God's existence and His power (Romans 1:20).

In Exodus 13:20-22, God provided a pillar of fire to give the Israelites light so they would be able to follow Him in the dark of night. The cloud by day and the pillar of fire by night reassured the people that God was with them leading them in the way they should go. The light made it possible for them to see their way rather than wander in darkness.

These Old Testament Scriptures give us a physical picture of a spiritual truth. When Jesus referred to Himself as Light He did not mean He was a physical light that shines like the sun, moon, or fire. He was communicating a spiritual truth about our world and His purpose in it.

The world was in total darkness before God provided light. Our world was engulfed in spiritual darkness because of sin. God provided the sun for our physical darkness and he provided Jesus for our spiritual darkness. Man can see and enter the kingdom of God and he can know God intimately. Jesus is the Light of the world!

purpose

I am the light of the world.   John 8:12

While I am in the world, I am the light of the world.   John 9:5

The true light that gives light to every man was coming into the world. To all who received him, to those who believed in his name, he gave the right to become children of God.   John 1:9,12

Scripture

Thank You, Jesus, for being the Light of the world. Thank You for bringing me out of spiritual darkness and into Your glorious light that I might have life! Let Your glory be seen in the earth as You open the eyes of people throughout the nations to Your love for them!

prayer

THE LIGHT OF THE WORLD (CONTINUED)

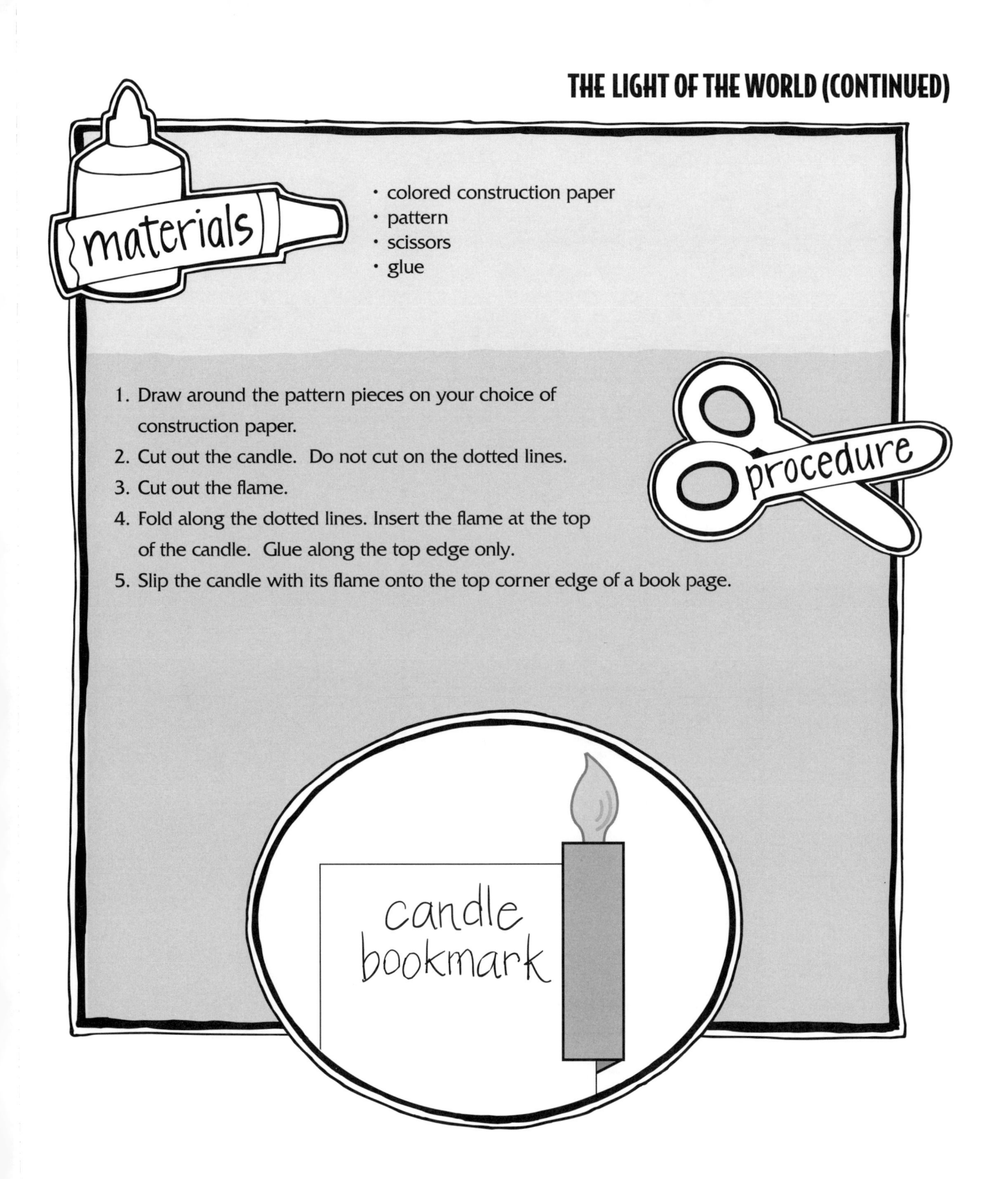

materials

- colored construction paper
- pattern
- scissors
- glue

procedure

1. Draw around the pattern pieces on your choice of construction paper.
2. Cut out the candle. Do not cut on the dotted lines.
3. Cut out the flame.
4. Fold along the dotted lines. Insert the flame at the top of the candle. Glue along the top edge only.
5. Slip the candle with its flame onto the top corner edge of a book page.

candle bookmark

PATTERNS FOR CANDLE BOOKMARK

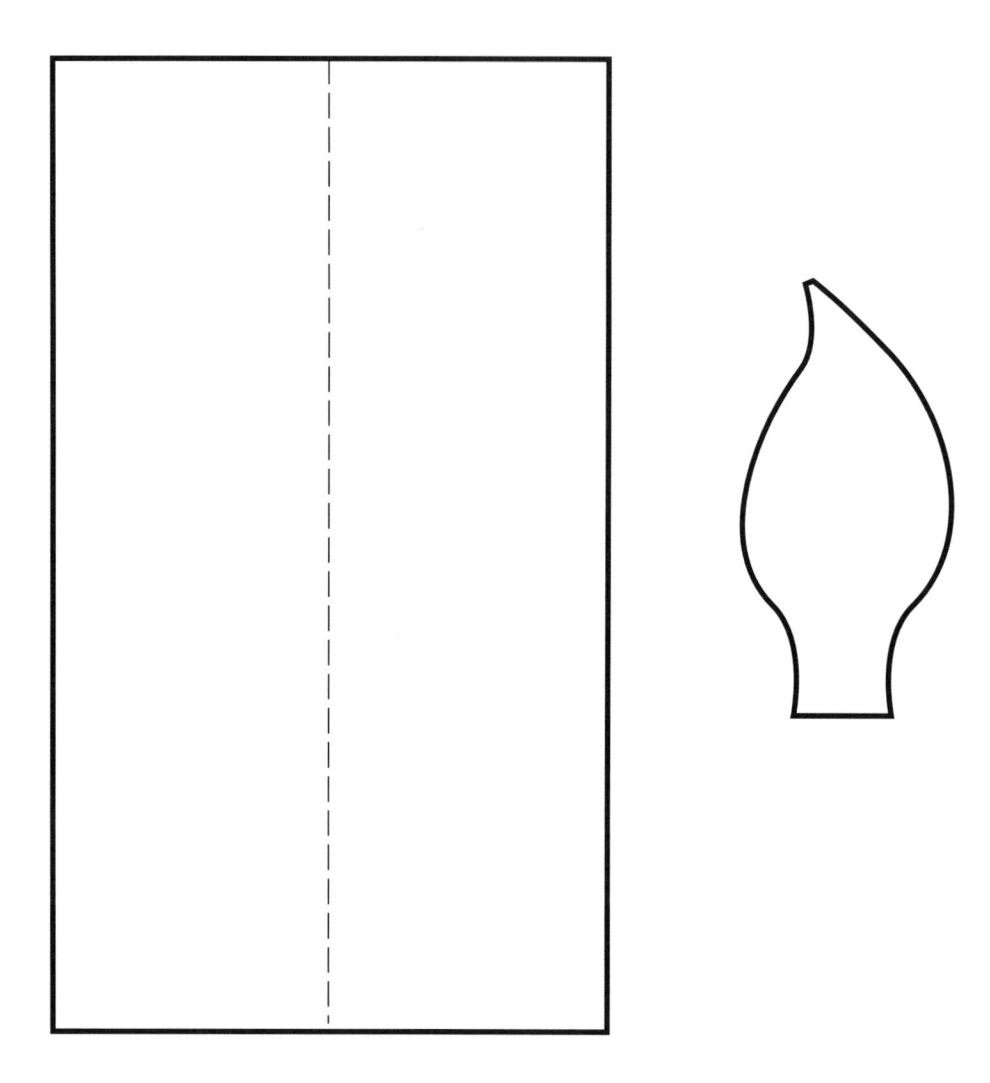

The True Vine

SCRIPTURE HANGING

Jesus is the true Vine. Read John 15:1-8.

Just as life giving elements flow out from the vine to the branches God's blessing flowed through the nation Israel and out to its individual people. In the Old Testament they were God's chosen people for they were in covenant with Him. Their relationship with God was based on the rituals and laws He gave them to live by. When they failed in obeying the law there were specific rituals to carry out so that their sins were covered temporarily and they could continue to enjoy God's presence and blessing in their lives.

When Jesus referred to Himself as the "true Vine" in the New Testament, He was introducing a spiritual truth to His disciples about God's relationship with mankind through Him. The old covenant would be replaced by a new and better covenant. Jesus was announcing that as the "true Vine" He would be the way through which God's grace and blessing would flow. Man could know God and enjoy His presence in their lives through Jesus Christ. He likens the care the gardener gives the vine to the work of the Holy Spirit in our lives.

A gardener will prune his vine regularly so that it will produce more and better quality fruit. Pruning is a process of removing dead branches to clean the plant and removing some live parts to improve its form and to increase it fruitfulness. The life force that resides in the vine can now flow efficiently into the branches.

Although the branches of the vine are weak, if they remain attached to the vine they will not only grow but with good care and patience they will produce good fruit. Just as the branches must be attached to the vine to grow and produce fruit so must the believer have a vital relationship with Jesus through His Word and prayer. As a result the Holy Spirit deals with our heart and "prunes" those things in our life that do not please Him. And, just as the weak branches receive life from the vine we in our weaknesses can change and grow by the power of the Holy Spirit working in us. With care and patience our lives will produce the fruit of God's Spirit and glorify Him.

I am the true vine, and my Father is the gardener. John 15:1

I am the vine; you are the branches. John. 15:5

Thank You, Jesus, that You are the true Vine and through You I receive not only eternal life but also the strength and power to live for God's glory! Thank You that Your Spirit lives and works in me to produce the fruit of Your Spirit!

THE TRUE VINE (CONTINUED)

materials

- ivy patterns
- sponge cloth (found in any grocery store)
- scissors or X-Acto knife
- pencil
- glue
- newspapers
- large spools of thread
- plastic wrap
- rubber band
- tempera paints: green, brown
- fine bristle & medium bristle brushes
- water
- paper towels
- small brown lunch bag
- fine tip black marker
- ruler
- 5" x 7" inexpensive wood or black frame

preparation

1. Cover the work space with newspaper and set out paints, brushes, paper towels, and water.
2. Place a small square of plastic wrap over the end of each large spool of thread and secure with rubber bands.

procedure

1. Draw around and cut out ivy patterns on sponge cloth. Use the X-acto knife to carefully cut vein lines.
2. Glue each ivy leaf to a covered spool of thread. Set aside.
3. Cut and spread out the small paper bag. Measure and mark a 5" x 7" section and cut it out.
4. Using a pencil and ruler neatly center and print in large letters on the 5" x 7" paper: "I am the true vine." John 15:1 Trace over the pencil with marker.
5. Take the paper to the painting table. Use one of the ivy spools and paint the leaf green.
6. Before you press and print the ivy leaf on the brown paper first print it on a paper towel to remove excess paint. Then print the leaf to the side of the verse. Repeat the procedure using each ivy spool and shades of paint to make a vine around the verse.
7. Using a fine tip bristle brush and brown paint lightly paint little stems connecting the ivy leaves. Dry.
8. Frame the verse.

SCRIPTURE HANGING PATTERNS

I am the true vine.

John 15:1

The Resurrection and the Life

DECORATED FLOWER POT

purpose

"Come forth!" spoke Jesus to the man who had been dead for four days. By the power and authority of the words Jesus spoke Lazarus came out of the grave alive!

Read the story of Lazarus in John 11.

When Jesus spoke of being the Resurrection and the Life He was introducing Martha to a deeper truth than just His ability to restore physical life. He was telling her that He is the source of all life and that anyone who would believe in Him could receive this life - even eternal life. Jesus was proclaiming the gospel! All those who put their faith in Jesus as their Savior are united with Him. This means that the same Spirit that raised Jesus from the dead now lives in each believer. What an assurance to our hearts when we realize that Jesus is the Resurrection and the Life!

Scripture

Jesus said to her, "I am the resurrection and the life. He who believes in me will live, even though he dies; and whoever lives and believes in me will never die." John 11:25

He (Jesus) became the source of eternal salvation. Hebrews 5:9

God has given us eternal life, and this life is in his Son. I John 5:11

The Son of God has come and has given us understanding, so that we may know him who is true. And we are in him who is true—even in his Son Jesus Christ. He is the true God and eternal life. I John 5:20

prayer

Thank You, Jesus, that You are life. Thank You for paying the price for my sin and sending Your Spirit to live in me that I, too, may have life—even eternal life!

SCIENCE EXTRA!

As a simple illustration for your discussion with your children, soak a lima bean seed between 2 damp paper towels until the outer shell is soft enough to remove. When it is soft, open the seed removing the outer shell and observe the tiny bean sprout within. Explain to your children that when the bean seed is buried in the soil the power of life within the bean sprout forces the outer shell to open and fall away releasing the bean sprout to live and grow. This is a picture of death for the believer. Death is a release, a door to pass through, to eternal life.

THE RESURRECTION AND THE LIFE (CONTINUED)

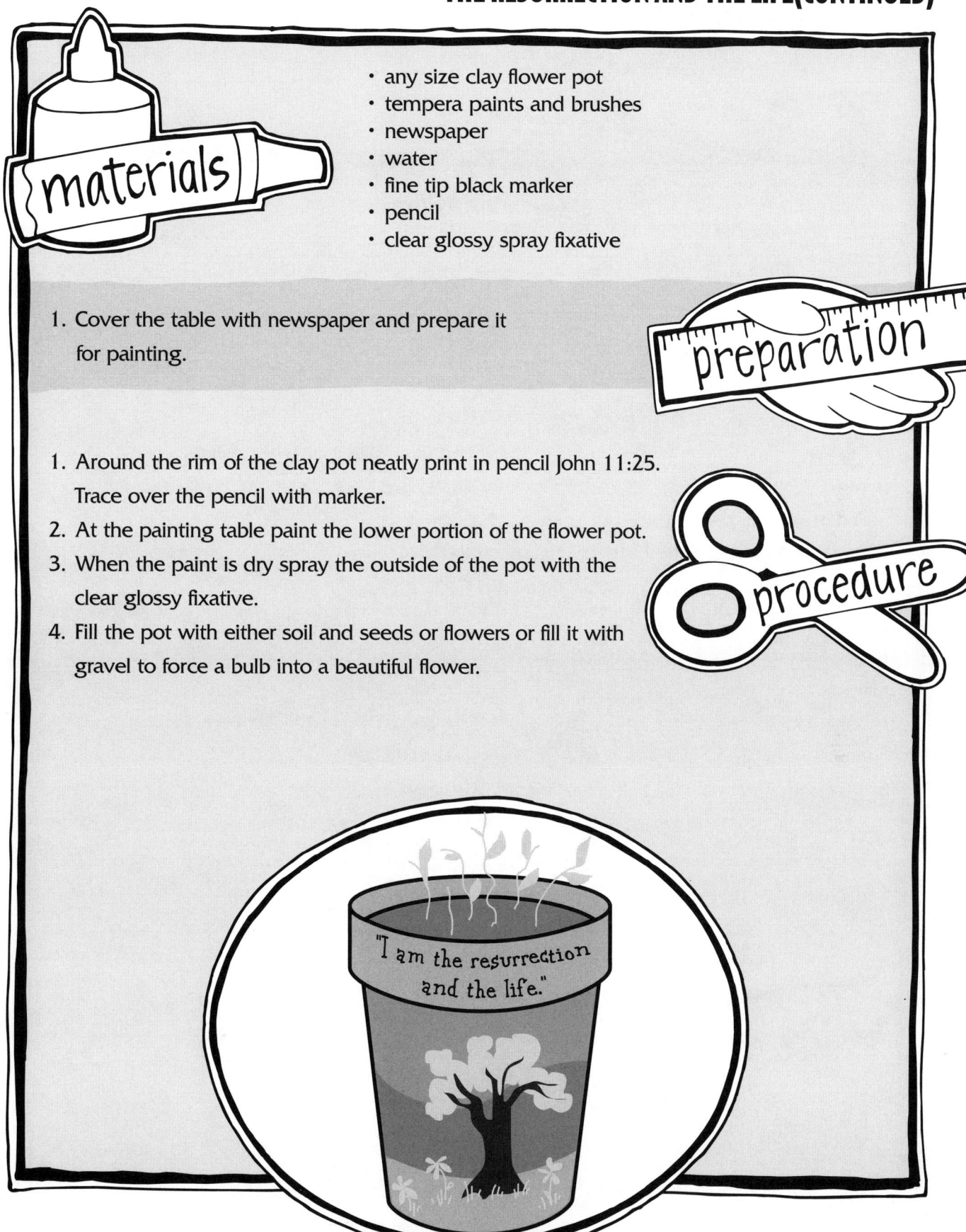

materials

- any size clay flower pot
- tempera paints and brushes
- newspaper
- water
- fine tip black marker
- pencil
- clear glossy spray fixative

preparation

1. Cover the table with newspaper and prepare it for painting.

procedure

1. Around the rim of the clay pot neatly print in pencil John 11:25. Trace over the pencil with marker.
2. At the painting table paint the lower portion of the flower pot.
3. When the paint is dry spray the outside of the pot with the clear glossy fixative.
4. Fill the pot with either soil and seeds or flowers or fill it with gravel to force a bulb into a beautiful flower.

The Bright and Morning Star

SUN CATCHER

purpose

Jesus is the Bright and Morning Star! Your children may wonder what significance there is in Jesus referring to Himself in Revelation 22:16 as "the Bright and Morning Star."

What star is visible in the day and is often referred to as the "morning star" or "day star"? The morning star or day star is the sun. The sun is not a planet, but a star! It is the nearest star to the earth at a distance of 93 million miles. Although it is 109 times the diameter of the earth it appears no larger than the moon in our sky because it is so far away. The sun is of great significance to the earth for without its heat and light there would be no life on earth.

The likeness of the sun or morning star to Jesus is thought provoking. Just as the sun sends out heat and light in its rays to maintain physical life on earth, the Father has sent His Son to show forth His glory, His mercy, and His love to us and give us life, even eternal life.

The faithfulness of the sun's rising and setting each day is a constant reminder of the faithfulness of our Lord Jesus. List five examples of His faithfulness. For help read: I John 1:9, I Corinthians 1:7-9, 2 Thessalonians 3:3, Laminations 3:22-23, and Psalm 100:5.

Finally, as the bright morning star rises each day it pushes back the darkness of night. Each day brings a new beginning and a new hope. When Jesus comes into a person's heart there is a new beginning as well

Let each child choose one Scripture used in the lesson to use in making this simple sun catcher for their window and serve as a reminder to them of Jesus, the Bright and Morning Star.

Scripture

I am the root and the offspring of David, and the bright and morning star. Revelation 22:16, KJV

The Son is the radiance of God's glory. Hebrews. 1:3

prayer

Thank You, Jesus, that You are the Bright and Morning Star. You give life, hope, and the power to live for You every day. You are faithful in every way!

THE BRIGHT AND MORNING STAR (CONTINUED)

materials

- yellow 9" plastic party plates
- scissors
- X-Acto knife, cutting board
- ruler
- pencil
- glue
- pattern
- paper punch
- white computer paper
- yellow crayons
- aluminum foil
- paper towels
- electric food warming tray
- oven mitts
- newspapers
- length of narrow ribbon
- black fine tip marker
- sun catcher hook

preparation

1. Cover the work space with newspapers.
2. Cover the food warming tray with foil over the tray edge.
3. Plug the food warming tray into an electric outlet and preheat at a low temperature.
4. Peel the paper wrap away from the yellow crayons.
5. Place the crayons and paper towels at the covered work space.
6. For younger children prepare the two plastic plates by cutting the center out with the X-Acto knife.

procedure

To make the transparent sun:
1. Draw around the sun pattern on the white computer paper.
2. Print child's name in the corner.
3. One child at a time comes to the work space and puts on the oven mitts.
4. Lay the sun drawing on the warm foil surface.
5. Using the yellow crayons completely color the sun. Notice how the crayon glides across the paper as the wax melts.
6. When the sun is a solid yellow remove it from the foil.
7. It will quickly dry. Cut out the sun.

(continued on pg. 44)

THE BRIGHT AND MORNING STAR (CONTINUED)

To make the sun catcher:

1. Older children can use the X-Acto knife to cut the centers of the plastic plates out or they can poke a hole in the center of both 9" plastic plates and then cut the entire centers out with scissors leaving only the rims.
2. With the two plates together mark and punch a hole in each rim.
3. Separate the plates. Lay one plate on the work surface.
4. Lay the cut out sun in the open center with the ray tips overlapping the plate rim. Glue the ray tips in place.
5. On the second plate's rim neatly print with the black marker across the top half of the rim "Jesus, the Bright and Morning Star."
6. Print neatly across the bottom half of the rim with the fine tip marker a Scripture of choice.
7. Lay the second plate inside the first covering the ray tips and matching the holes of both plates. Glue in place.
8. Pull the length of narrow ribbon through the hole in the plates and tie a bow. Hang in a window on a sun catcher hook.

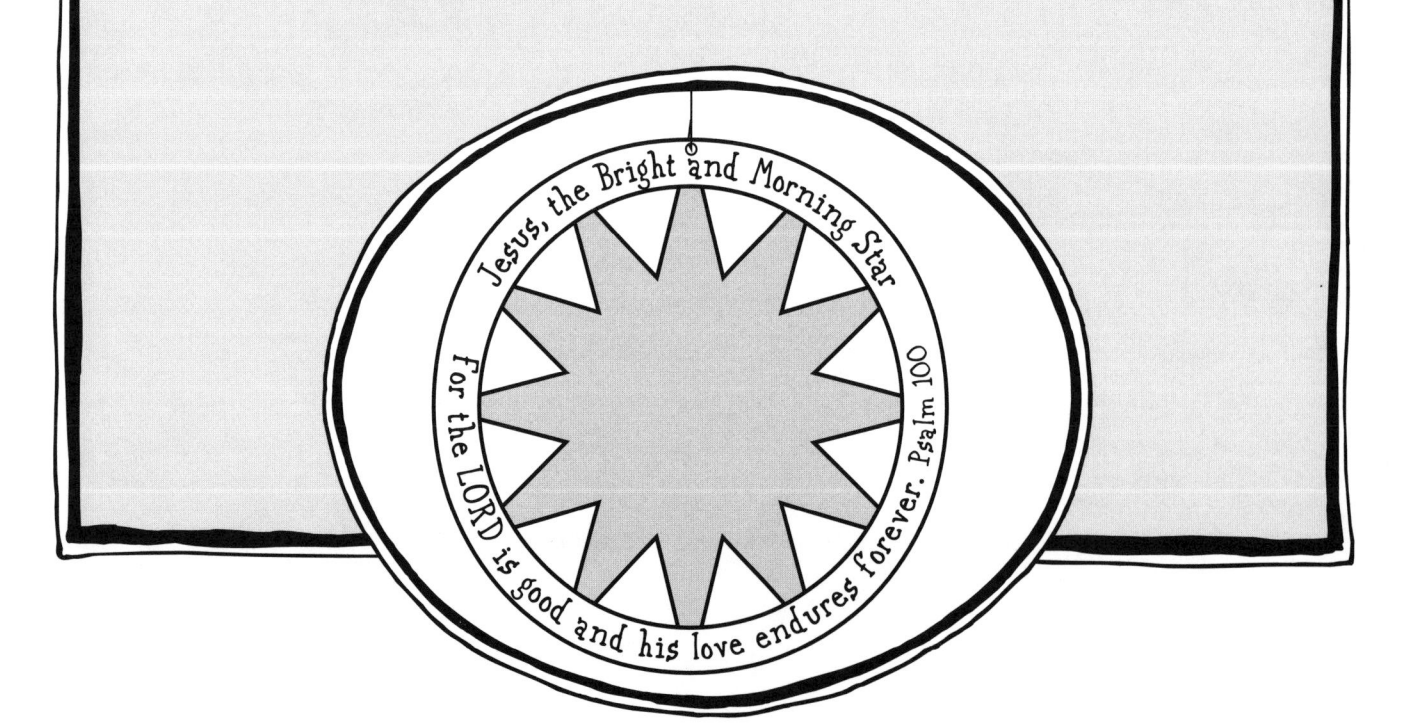

MORNING STAR PATTERN

The Way, the Truth, and the Life

DOILY HANGING

"How can we know the way?" Thomas asked Jesus.

Although Thomas had spent time with Jesus listening to His instruction and observing His life and ministry, he had little understanding of Jesus' teachings. Read John 14:1-6. Thomas was a man longing to know and understand the things Jesus spoke about and he was not afraid to ask when he did not grasp their meaning.

Jesus understood Thomas' question as sincere earnestness to understand the things of God. Jesus responds to Thomas by saying "I am the way, the truth, and the life. No one comes to the Father except through Me."

Jesus told Thomas that He was THE Way not A way to the Father and to heaven. Jesus is the only way.

Jesus told Thomas that He is the Truth. Thomas was a seeker of truth. He had a heart searching and longing for truth and he found his answer in Jesus. Jesus is the source of truth.

Jesus told Thomas that He is the Life. Jesus is the source of life. By His Spirit He quickens the heart of a sinner to life, reveals the truth of the gospel to bring conviction and repentance, and shows him the way by leading him to God through believing and trusting in Jesus as Savior. Jesus surely is the way, the truth, and the life!

purpose

Scripture

Jesus answered, "I am the way and the truth and the life. No one comes to the Father except through me." John 14:6

By the blood of Jesus, by a new and living way... let us draw near to God. Hebrews 10:19,22

Truth came through Jesus Christ. John 1:17

In Him (Jesus) was life. John 1:4

Thank You, Jesus, for leading me and providing the way for me to know God, my Father. You revealed the truth of the gospel to me by Your Spirit and You quickened my heart to respond to that truth. Thank You that I am no longer dead in my sins but I have been made alive by Your life that now dwells in me!

prayer

THE WAY, THE TRUTH, AND THE LIFE (CONTINUED)

materials

- 10" diameter or larger paper lace doily
- 5" diameter embroidery hoop
- 1 yard 1/4" wide satin ribbon
- fine tip colored markers
- ruler
- newspaper

procedure

1. Lay the paper doily on a sheet of newspaper. In the center of the paper doily neatly print John 14:6 with a colored marker.
2. Use the colored markers to color in the designs on the paper doily.
3. Center the doily on top of the inner embroidery hoop.
4. Snap the outer hoop over the inner hoop. The Scripture verse should be in the center and readable.
5. Measure, cut, and glue a length of 1/4" wide ribbon on the embroidery hoop rim.
6. Use the remainder of satin ribbon to tie a bow over the embroidery hoop fastener. Hang in a window or on a door.

CHECK WITH YOUR LOCAL CHRISTIAN BOOK STORE FOR THESE OTHER EXCITING EDUCATIONAL RESOURCES!

Other arts and crafts resources for ages 6 and up:
Celebrate the Holidays with Scripture	0805402454
Celebrate God's Word About Me	0805402470
Celebrate Learning About God and His Word	0805402462
Celebrate Walking with Jesus	0805402489
Celebrate the World God Made	0805408266

Academic activity books:
Red Letter Days, Special Activities and Devotions for Every Letter of the Alphabet (Preschool)	0805402349
God Made You Sense-ational, Special Activities for Teaching the 5 Senses (Ages 5-10)	0805402357
Address: Planet Earth	080540824X
Off to Work We Go	0805408231

Science experiments that point elementary-age children to the Creator!
The Glad Scientist Discovers the Creator	0805402640
The Glad Scientist Visits Outer Space	0805402659
The Glad Scientist Learns About the Weather	0805408304
The Glad Scientist Explores the Human Body	0805408290

Coloring Books for children of all ages:
Ancient Heroes - Noah	0805400443
Ancient Heroes - Moses	0805400451
Ancient Heroes - Esther	080540046X
Ancient Heroes - David and the Leaders of Israel	0805400478

Teaching Posters books:
Big Book of Teaching Posters: Community Helpers	0805402667
Big Book of Teaching Posters: Nature	0805402675
Inspirational Poster Book for Children	0805402683

Classroom Poster sets:
Days of the Week and The Months of the Year	0805404201
Numbers and The Alphabet	0805404198
Set an Example and Why Study?	0805404244
Plan of Salvation and The Golden Rule	080540421X
The Ten Commandments and The Lord's Prayer	0805404236
Fruit of the Spirit and Armor of God	0805404228
Colors and Shapes	0805406093
Psalm 23 and Jesus Loves Me	0805406107
Books of the Old Testament and the New Testament	0805406115
Food Pyramid and Five Senses	0805406123